A LITTLE BOOK OF UNKNOWING

This little book of unknowing is hugely powerful in its scope, beauty and profound articulation of complex aspects of the spiritual journey of unknowing. The integration of Jennifer's own experiences with her deep noetic knowing of unknowing threaded through spiritual wisdom from well-known spiritual teachers is exquisite. I highly recommend this work to both experienced seekers and beginners – both can learn and grow from such a well of wisdom.

Rev Dr Lynne Sedgmore, OBE, Ordained Interfaith Minister, Spiritual Director and retreat leader

A book that insists we accept a simple, yet profound truth – how little we actually know. It insists because through embracing the mystery of existence, hidden doorways to spiritual liberation are revealed.

An ancient approach to spiritual exploration, rediscovered for the modern age. An important book that will help many people.

Rev Simon Small, Chaplain, Abbey House Retreat Centre, Glastonbury

The teachings on prayer, on passivity, on patience and waiting, on the importance of openness and trust and the very real need to recognize how we enslave ourselves by our impulses, are excellent. It also introduces some unique ideas about formlessness and the power to make grace work in the moment.

Such a special, helpful and very much-needed book for this uncertain time.

Lucinda M. Vardey, editor of *The Twelve Degrees of Silence*

A Little Book
of Unknowing

A Little Book
of Unknowing

Jennifer Kavanagh

CHRISTIAN
ALTERNATIVE

Winchester, UK
Washington, USA

First published by Christian Alternative Books, 2015
Christian Alternative Books is an imprint of John Hunt Publishing Ltd.,
Laurel House, Station Approach,
Alresford, Hants, SO24 9JH, UK
office1@jhpbooks.net
www.johnhuntpublishing.com
www.christian-alternative.com

For distributor details and how to order please visit the 'Ordering' section on our website.

Text copyright: Jennifer Kavanagh 2014

ISBN: 978 1 78279 808 8
Library of Congress Control Number: 2014954855

A CIP catalogue record for this book is available from the British Library.

Design: Lee Nash

Printed and bound by CPI Group (UK) Ltd, Croydon, CR0 4YY, UK

We operate a distinctive and ethical publishing philosophy in all
areas of our business, from our global network of authors to
production and worldwide distribution.

CONTENTS

By the same author

The Methuen Book of Animal Tales (ed.)
The Methuen Book of Humorous Stories (ed.)
Call of the Bell Bird
The World is our Cloister
New Light (ed.)
Journey Home (formerly The O of Home)
Simplicity Made Easy
Small Change, Big Deal
The Failure of Success

Fiction
The Emancipation of B

References
All the references in the text are to the books and editions in
Further Reading and Resources.

For Lucinda

Help me to be quiet, to sit here
...slowly unknowing everything,
Becoming dark, becoming yielding,
Just sitting.

Gunilla Norris

I

Introduction

There is no certainty, fixity or isolation in nature.

Iain McGilchrist

Certainty is a comfortable position. It's a place to retire to, a protective cloak against the vagaries of the world. We are all drawn to it, but for some it is more important than others. In the sphere of spirituality, those who seek certainty will be attracted to religions with a well-defined structure and clear creedal system rather than what they might regard as the "wishy-washy" more experientially based faiths.

Certainty, we learn, is a left-brain quality, associated with rigidity, and an inability to see the wider picture, understand, connect, or empathise with someone who holds a different opinion. The left hemisphere tends to see things in isolation, without the tempering quality that the right brain provides.

In people with a predominantly left-brain disposition, certainty will be not so much an attraction as a defining characteristic: a shield to repel all boarders. In the religious sphere, this applies equally to the religious fundamentalist and the hardened atheist. A path that cherishes uncertainty will not, of course, be attractive to either.

The concept of unknowing is best known from *The Cloud of Unknowing*, a little book by an anonymous fourteenth-century author, but it has its roots in the earlier and influential Dionysius the Areopagite, and in the austere spirituality of the fourth-century Desert Fathers and Mothers. It is at the heart of what is called the *via negativa*, an approach to God through emptiness, through a stripping away of concepts or images, through an acceptance of the fallibility of

1

the ego-driven life.

This is not a book about theology or a particular religion. Its frame of reference is a faith-filled life that is available to all, a way that has endured for millennia, and is often referred to as "The Perennial Philosophy". Nor is it an in-depth book about mysticism but a little book about a particular way of being in the world.

The way we run our lives is dependent on what we know of the world, and we have expectations and make assumptions accordingly. But what if the facts on which we base our lives are shown to be unreliable? What if our expectations are confounded? Then, what if we let go of our familiar, habitual ways of thinking? What if we let go of those assumptions and expectations? What if we let go of the very need to know? The sense of release might surprise us. The opportunity is there.

In this book we will explore what we think we know, and what we don't know, what we can and can't know. We will look at the nature of our knowing, and how letting go of a limited kind of knowing will open us to a fuller, richer experience. We will consider how we can lead our lives with an understanding that there is much that we do not know; and how we might be able to experiment with spaciousness and leave room for the creative energy of the Spirit. We will see how by practice and attention we can move into an acceptance of unknowing, and deepen our experience of life, love and the Divine.

At the end of each chapter are given a couple of questions arising from the text. These may be useful for individual reflection, or for discussion in a group.

Maybe I should offer some possible definitions that relate to key terms used in the book.

Spirituality is simply a question of having an open enough mind to see that there are things in the world at large that transcend what we can know and fully comprehend, that are not fully accounted for in a reductionist, materialist account (Rowson and McGilchrist, 42).

The philosopher and psychologist William James describes the religious attitude in the soul thus:

Were one asked to characterise the life of religion in the broadest and most general terms possible, one might say that it consists of the belief that there is an *unseen order*, and that our supreme good lies in harmoniously adjusting ourselves thereto (53).

And of mysticism Evelyn Underhill wrote:

Broadly speaking, I understand it to be the expression of the innate tendency of the human spirit towards complete harmony with the transcendent order: whatever the theological order be under which that order is understood (xiv).

But let us start with the processes of our everyday world.

2

The need to know

I took a test in existentialism. I left all the answers blank and got 100.

Woody Allen

We have such a need to acquire knowledge, to find out, such a hungry need to know. All the emphasis of modern education and life in general is on the rational acquisition of factual knowledge. Ignorance, not knowing, is uncomfortable; we feel it puts us at a disadvantage.

The unreliability of facts

Facts are a mainstay of our understanding of the world. Historical, geographical, sociological and scientific – every part of our lives can be factually described: where we live, how old we are, how many legs a millipede has, when Julius Caesar conquered Britain. Where, when, how many – we seek for concrete absolutes.

The human capacity for learning, for retention of what we have learnt, is vast. Individually and as a species, we have created and are constantly expanding a vast store-house of knowledge in our brains, on paper, and in all media so far discovered. Trillions of volumes, files, and research papers. We have a phenomenal capacity for knowledge.

And it's something by which we rightly set great store. We test and examine each other; education and careers depend on it. Some subjects more than others are reliant on retention of facts, but the large audiences for quizzes on radio and television demonstrate how much we love testing our knowledge, both general and specialist. Given our dependence on and interest in facts, it's hard to accept that not all facts are reliable. Using the phrase "the half-life of facts", medical students are apparently told that half of what they learn will, in ten or twenty years' time, be found to be untrue. "Facts" are dependent on the current state of human knowledge: they are provisional, best guesses at any given moment. It has even been said that there is no such thing as a fact.

What to believe?

We are bombarded by research, the findings of which are often contradictory. In medicine, in economics, from all the "facts" so confidently asserted on the media and on our screens, how do we know which to believe? The awkward truth is that many findings heralded as breakthroughs have never been re-tested, and of those that have, many have been found to be false (see Wolff).

Even facts that we might accept as reliably proven aren't always helpful in isolation. In order to understand what we are being taught, we need context, and that's not generally part of the package.

We might also remember that many things confidently expressed as facts are determined by subjectivity. We cannot say what someone else sees as red, or what they hear when they listen to Mendelssohn's *Elijah* or the song of a thrush. In fact, as Rebecca Pisciotta writes in her blog, the subjectivity of experience is more extensive:

> Research in a wide range of fields has touched upon the nature of subjectivity... If we compile the ideas gleaned from physics, neuroscience, research on memory, and the human experience we can begin to form a more comprehensive picture of the nature and depth of the subjective experience. The picture shows us that: individuals actually experience physically different realities, their sensory

experience is at the neural level processed differently, different mental representations of reality are thus obtained, reality is consciously experienced differently, individuals remember different realities, and that they remember their memories differently.
http://serendip.brynmawr.edu/exchange/node/365

Even the reliability of our familiar objects has let us down. We now learn that a table or a wall might not really be "there" in any permanent way. The matter in the universe, we are told, is made of waves in empty space. All the "material" properties of matter and its fields are only appearances. The world is an illusion. All of a sudden, science seems to be speaking with a Buddhist voice:

> An atom has no inherent nature... an atom has no essence of its own... the atom has no intrinsic nature so it is empty.
> 7th century Chinese philosopher, Fa-Tsang, (in Mitchell, 47-49)

Questions

- What do you know?
- How do you let go of certainty?

3

Expectation

I really expect little or nothing from the future. Certainly not great "experiences" or a lot of interesting new things. Maybe, but so what? What really intrigues me is the idea of starting out into something unknown, demanding and expecting nothing very special, hoping only to do what God asks of me, whatever it may be.

Thomas Merton

We not only feel impelled to know, we have an expectation of knowing and, with our human arrogance, we convince ourselves we can know everything. Indeed, from childhood on we seem predisposed to think that we *do* know. However often our expectations are dashed, we confidently plan our work, our life, as if we were omniscient. Have we forgotten the name of our species? *Homo sapiens,* not *homo omnisciens.* A wise species we may be, but not an all-knowing one. As Socrates said: "The only true wisdom is in knowing you know nothing."

Our assumption of omniscience is part of a linear, time-dependent way of thinking and living. Progress is sequential – "and then, and then" rules our lives. We live much of those lives in the future tense. We plan what we will do tomorrow or after work today. We write "to-do" lists, make resolutions for the New Year. We plan where our children (sometimes as yet unborn) will go to school. We have diaries full of future engagements. In business, there are five-year plans, and staff appraisals asking: "Where do you see yourself in three years' time?"

Life and death

Our assumptions about the future come from an expectation that we know what will happen, or even that we can control it. But every now and then we are reminded of the unpredictability of the universe. We have only to look at careful lives devastated by earthquake or civil war; at well-managed careers changed for ever by cancer or a car accident. Plans and their expected outcomes can be dashed by the unexpected. Life gets in the way.

Death too. We don't know how we will die – unless we are already sick and the end is nigh. We don't know when – it might be in thirty years, it might be tomorrow, or a terminally ill patient might live years beyond their prognosis. And we don't know what, if anything, will happen afterwards. That is, unless some personal experience has given us some indication. Some people say they remember their past lives; some accounts of near-death experiences seem to point to a kind of commonality. Part of living with not knowing is taking death in our stride as part of the world we do not know.

Based on probability and previous experience, there's a certain amount that we can forecast, but often the timing of, for instance, weather patterns, is hard to gauge. And some things come out of the blue. Although there may sometimes be some indications of probability, we can't usually predict human error or mischief, the advent of a computer virus, an earthquake, or the moment a baby is conceived.

Whether we see these life events as caused by chance, destiny, an interventionist God or the working of the universe, there's no denying that they occur. The unexpected, though barely acknowledged, actually absorbs quite a lot of our attention. We set up risk assessments in an attempt to second-guess the future. Taking out an insurance policy is in itself an acknowledgement of life's unpredictability. Interestingly, "acts of God" are generally excluded from insurance cover, in itself a recognition that some events are beyond our imaginings. Superstition is a less conscious and more fearful response to the uncertainties of life. Not walking under a ladder may be classed as a sensible precaution; not walking on the cracks in the pavement, throwing spilt salt over our shoulder, however lightly or habitually undertaken, are reactions to unnamed but often physically imagined fears, comparable to the night-time imaginings of a child.

Why do we get upset when weather or a technological failure interferes with our plans? That's just how life is. Why do we complain, full stop? Problematic circumstances are either something we have the power to change, or not. In either case, complaint is pointless. Hackneyed though it may have become, the Serenity Prayer has some point: "God grant me the serenity to accept the things I cannot change, the courage to change the things I can, and the wisdom to know the difference."

In the complexities of our lives we rely on so many interweaving factors; in our bodies we rely on the thousands of separate muscles, nerves and cells. It's not surprising if one of them – a tooth, a joint – sometimes lets us down. In the intricate dance of all the beings of the world, it's not surprising if our own small path is sometimes inconvenienced.

Even on a journey where there are no diversions, no replacement buses, no cancelled flights, what we have planned is only the tip of the iceberg. Even when life does proceed in an orderly fashion and according to our expectations, a lot more happens along the way. Even if we know the route we are going to tread, we don't know what we might meet as we go, the encounters we might have, the bird or insect we might hear, what we might find on our path. And incidental events or meetings may have a much more significant and long-lasting impact than those we expected. Some of the richest experiences in my life have come from encounters with strangers – on trains or planes. As Martin Buber says, "All journeys have secret destinations of which the traveller is unaware."

The unexpected

The unexpected not only plays a large part in our lives, it is so much more *interesting* than what we expect. When we open ourselves to the richness and joy of the unexpected, we notice so much more: a man riding a Penny Farthing bicycle in central London; a group of school children running along the street with swimming towels over their heads to protect them from the rain; a man juggling as he waits to cross the road. What such experiences call out in us is also unexpected: a lurch of joy or of sadness, an unexpected tear or memory.

How our lives develop is unpredictable; career advisors' horizons are limited, and so are our imaginations. We often end up doing things we had never dreamt of, let alone planned. Some of the jobs I have done in my life I had never even heard of ten years before. If anyone had told me twenty years ago that I would have done some of the things I have done in the last fifteen, I would never have believed them.

We cannot know either how we will react in a given situation; we do not know until we are faced with it. We might imagine fear or heroics – the reality is often different. People who risk their lives to save or comfort a stranger talk of obeying a natural impulse, of having no choice. The moment brings its own truth and calls out from us an often unsuspected response.

Expectation is both misleading and limiting. For me, creative growth is learning that there is much that I do not know, and trying to let go of my forward-looking compulsion.

Questions

- How do you plan?
- How do you open yourself to the unexpected?

4

Not knowing

To come to the knowledge of all
desire the knowledge of nothing

St John of the Cross

If we accept the limitation of our knowledge, where does that get us?

Much has been made of the difference, indeed the opposition, of religion and science. But the more we hear of modern scientific research, especially in physics, the closer they seem to be. Contrary to popular belief, science is not about establishing indisputable facts, it is about positing and attempting to prove (or disprove) hypotheses, with the understanding that any discovery may be superseded in the future. Science is about a spirit of enquiry. The unknown is accepted, even welcomed as a challenge for future research. As biologist Stuart Firestein said, "What we don't know is our job. It's much more interesting to think about what we don't know than what we do know." That too is the mystic position.

But, whereas scientists may see this place as a challenge to learn more and to eradicate more areas of uncertainty, for mystics or spiritual seekers, the challenge may be about embracing that uncertainty, about accepting that for some questions there will be no answers – and that *it doesn't matter*. Not only that it doesn't matter but that the unforeseen may contain riches that go beyond what in our habitual ways of thinking and in our workaday lives we are capable of imagining. In giving the unforeseen more of a chance, we are opening up opportunities for our creative selves, for spontaneity, for the part of us that goes beyond the routine certainties of everyday life.

If we recognise that it is the unforeseen that might have the most importance in our lives, we may allow ourselves to welcome uncertainty. Welcoming uncertainty, embracing it, does not mean commending ignorance or trying not to know; it's not about the rejection of knowledge. It's not about the negation of the intellect, but its enhancement. It is a recognition that cognitive thinking cannot reach everything, an understanding that the scientific and spiritual approaches are not incompatible, just different, complementary, dimensions. Not either/or but both/and.

* * *

To know is not a simple act. In other languages there are separate words to suggest different kinds of knowing. In French, for instance, *savoir* is used to indicate knowledge of facts; *connaître* means to know in a deeper way: to be acquainted with a person or a place. Knowing in this latter sense is an act not merely of the brain but indicates an experience that might take place on many levels.

When we say we know someone in the sense of being acquainted with them, we may not rely greatly on the facts about them – their height, age, the colour of their hair – but on subjective qualities, how they seem to us – friendly, reserved or outspoken. And if acquaintance ripens into friendship, what is important is the quality of our relationship, how we respond to each other, what we share emotionally. But can we say that we actually *know* anyone else? Even our life partner? There is always a private portion of their inmost being that is inaccessible to anyone else. Do we know ourselves? Do we know the essential self beneath the personality pasted on for the outside world, beyond the identities we assume in the different roles in our lives? As we know from all the therapeutic and self-help books, getting to know ourselves is a lifetime's journey.

If we don't know those whom we can see, touch, talk to and encounter with our minds and senses, nor ourselves with whom we live all the time, how can we expect to know something beyond ourselves, a hidden power, the Divine? How can we know God?

Questions

- What questions don't have answers?
- How do you know yourself?

5

Another way of knowing

In contemplation God teaches the soul very quietly and secretly, without its knowing how, without the sound of words, and without the help of any bodily or spiritual faculty, in silence and in quietude, in darkness to all sensory and natural things.

St John of the Cross, *The Spiritual Canticle*

On my mother's Kindle is a list of the titles and authors of the books downloaded on it. For The Bible the authors are listed as "God *et al*." Apart from enjoying the presumably unintentional humour, I appreciate the recognition of the multi-authorship of the Bible, and its inspiration. Research has revealed a little of its authors, but can discover nothing of its inspiration, except as revealed in the experience of those who wrote it.

"God" is a word which for many provokes discomfort, echoes of an authoritarian judgmental deity, or a childhood perception of a bearded old man on a cloud. Many who reject any idea of the Divine are living with a concept which most of us would consider outdated. In answer to a theist's question: "Who is this God that you don't believe in?" the answer might not be so different from the view held by the questioner.

We all know that religion is sometimes viewed as a cross between superstition and an insurance policy, providing a comfort blanket or some kind of guarantee. And maybe there is some truth in that view of the certainties of particular religions, but faith is another matter. Faith is not about certainty, but about trust. If we could prove it we would not need faith.

We have seen that there is little about which we can be

certain. Certainty may be undermined by limitations of the current state of knowledge; the subjective nature of experience; the fluid quality of the material world; or the intervention of unforeseen events. But beyond these aspects of the world about which we often assume knowledge, there is a dimension of life to which rational explanation simply doesn't apply. Most people would admit that there is much that we cannot apprehend through reason or through the senses. We might know a fact with our brains, but not be able to understand what it means, to fully experience its reality – the age of a star or the trillions of connections within the human brain – some things are too big, too complex, for us to conceive. Einstein, who knew a thing or two about factual knowledge, felt that "imagination is more important than knowledge". There is a dimension which co-exists with the material, rationally grounded world, is not in opposition to it or threatened by scientific development but happily stands alone in the context of everything else. This is the world of religious experience.

Knowing God?

Jocelyn Bell Burnell is an astrophysicist. She is also a Quaker, a woman of faith, and is happy to hold the two aspects of her life in equilibrium. Like most scientists she is frank about the large areas of the world that remain unexplained. She is dismissive, however, about any concept of a God that fills in the gaps in human knowledge, for instance about what came before the Big Bang. She does not believe in "a God of the gaps". Her spiritual experience, she says, is on a different level, and she does not find the two incompatible. When she talks of her spiritual life, it is not with the certainty of the distinguished scientist, but the moving humility of someone who has received the grace of religious experience.

Traditionally there have been two approaches to God. One

is by the *via positiva*: by which God is celebrated, affirmed, described, in terms that lend themselves to a view of God in human or super-human terms. The other, the *via negativa*, asserts that God is beyond description, unknowable by the rational mind. This is the path of unknowing.

This apophatic tradition has been traced back to the fourth century, but was first named as such in the sixth by Dionysius the Areopagite, himself a profound influence on the author of *The Cloud*. It posits that we cannot know the ultimate mystery, the ultimate unknown: the nature of God. Any attempt to define or describe God is to distort, to impose our own limitations of time and space. Although we can ascribe to God such qualities as good, true and loving, we have to recognise that these are mere pointers, and we might want to learn to think of God without adjectives. The word "God" itself is a pointer to something beyond our description.

Not knowing is not the same as doubt (though they may co-exist). We may not know what, how or why, but our not knowing may co-exist with a firm knowledge *that*! And where does that knowledge come from? It comes from a different kind of knowing. A knowing that comes from experience.

My own experience is that faith took me by surprise. I was overwhelmed by an insistent inner call. I had no idea what was going on but it would not be denied. As for many others, faith came upon me in the wake of trauma, not as any kind of crutch, not as anything that came from my will, but as a new challenge in my life, a new dimension that in my newly cracked open state I was able to access. It took the form of an invitation – indeed, a requirement – to be myself, to be true to an inner voice, the voice of the Spirit. It meant listening, letting go of the need to control, and allowing my life to be guided. The self that emerged was new and fragile; for months I felt as if I were treading on eggshells, not wanting to talk to anyone, not wanting my social self to trample on these shoots of growth. I didn't know what was happening, but I was in a changed state.

Religious experiences, regardless of the faith label attached to them, have an extraordinary commonality. At the level of belief and of religious observance and rituals, the differences between the major world faiths are not to be disputed. But at the mystic level, differences disappear. When giving talks on mysticism I sometimes read pieces from different traditions and challenge the audience to name the religions from which they come. The similarities are such that they cannot do so. Take, for example, the following:

"Who says that Spirit is not known, knows; who claims that he knows, knows nothing."

And:

"There is in the mind no knowledge of God except the knowledge that it does not know Him."

These are from the Upanishads and St Augustine respectively.

The commonality between different religious experiences has often been described: by Aldous Huxley in *The Perennial Philosophy*, by Evelyn Underhill in her *Mysticism*, and in the ground-breaking book, *The Varieties of Religious Experience*, in which William James points out four qualities common to all mystic experiences, one of which is that they are "ineffable", that is, that they cannot be described. As the author of *The Cloud of Unknowing* explains, both the process and the aim are clouded in mystery: "It is not your will or desire that moves you, but something you are completely ignorant of stirring you to will and desire you know not what."

That does not mean that we cannot in some sense know God. The strange fact, as James discovered from his research, is that all such experiences are "noetic", that is, they bear an intrinsic quality of knowing. This is not the knowing of the rational mind, not a knowing limited to facts and practicalities based on the senses, or information derived from the senses, but a knowing that encompasses the entire being. Some consider that this deep knowing is something that we have known before: "The longing to be in touch with this 'knowing' arises from our origin when we knew of our 'being' and of being one with the creative energy and with all creation; we long to get back to this deep 'knowing'" (Jarman, 11).

For this profound kind of knowing, the *Cloud* author asserts that knowing the why and how will be more of a hindrance than a help. Only when we let go of the need to know in a cognitive sense are we able to access this new kind of knowing. If we set aside our rational priorities, and trust our experience and inner rather than outward certainty, we may discover a different, intuitive, quality. As we move into the realm of the heart and open it, as we open ourselves up to the vast unknown, launching ourselves into the void, placing ourselves into a place of ultimate vulnerability and ultimate trust, we find ourselves in a state from which that deeper knowing arises.

Questions

- How do you experience faith?
- How do you know God?

6

Another way of living

I am open to the guidance of synchronicity and do not let expectations hinder my path.

The Dalai Lama

And what about action in the world? How do we live our lives? If we start from a premise that we do not/cannot know everything that will happen, how do we move forward, how do we make decisions? After many decades of priding myself on my decisiveness, I was surprised, no, overwhelmed, to find myself in a different place. I found that the way forward was not a question of making decisions, but of allowing things to unfold, realising that matters would become clear. It was not a cerebral understanding, but an understanding reached, as in most spiritual development, in the act itself. Realising that I needed to give up the career of some thirty years, and with considerable preparation to safeguard my clients, I sold my business. I had no idea of what I would do, *and it didn't matter*. The necessity that impelled me and the freedom that awaited me combined to make it one of the most powerful spiritual experiences of my life so far. Why had it taken me so long to understand that this was the way to live my life? I became aware – it became clear – that I no longer needed to know.

Letting go

That first time was so liberating. It was not a decision, not something that came from my will, but an inward release. How had I not realised the enormous relief of surrendering my will to make things happen, and resting in the faith that it would be shown? It *has* been shown and continues to be so. As with all lessons in life, it is an ongoing one.

How it is shown is through the guidance of the Spirit, either directly or through others. In prayer or meditation, we centre ourselves in silence. In a collective experience, such as a Quaker Meeting for Worship, with an intense awareness not only of potential Presence but of the others in the room, we gather and we wait. We empty ourselves, both to bring ourselves into a state of awareness, and to listen for guidance about how we are to be in the world, what it is that we are being led to do. This is a time of worship and of discernment.

Synchronicity

In taking times of quiet, of prayer, a gut certainty will enable us to begin a course of action. Beginnings are important:

> Until one is committed, there is hesitancy, the chance to draw back, always ineffectiveness. Concerning all acts of initiative and creation, there is one elementary truth the ignorance of which kills countless ideas and splendid plans: that the moment one definitely commits oneself, then providence moves too. All sorts of things occur to help one that would never otherwise have occurred. A whole stream of events issues from the decision, raising in one's favour all manner of unforeseen incidents, meetings and material assistance which no man could have dreamed would have come his way. Whatever you can do or dream you can, begin it. Boldness has genius, power and magic in it. Begin it now.
>
> (Attributed to Goethe)

What we supply is the intention, and then we look for confirmation, which may come in many forms: sometimes from a phone call or a suggestion from another. These events, incidents and material assistance are often called synchronicity – seeming coincidences which are glimpses of an existing connection, hitherto unnoticed. The more open we are, the more these seem to appear. Synchronicity, said a friend, is "a conspiracy of grace". Or, as Einstein put it, "Coincidence is God's way of remaining anonymous."

A former director of a London charity, who has spent most of his life in giving service to the community, told me that his decision-making process is governed by his faith; guidance comes from synchronicity. "You get an idea of what is called for from a combination of influences around you." You don't need to understand it, he says;

> all you need to know is that you choose to interpret your experience and whether you can trust it. If there are several coincidences, and the idea doesn't leave you, you begin to believe you're on to something. It owns you. You must then ramp up your efforts and energies in that field. That's when you go for it. It's full on. You're done for!

This has certainly been my experience. About fifteen years ago, I spent a year travelling round the world. Before I went I had been volunteering for a charity that worked with street homeless people, and had found that many of the people we were working with had come out of prison. On my return from my travels I felt strongly that I was being called to work with prisoners, to help prevent them being homeless on release. But I had no idea how to go about it.

Someone mentioned that the Prison Reform Trust might appreciate some voluntary help.

So I planned to email them but the following morning picked up a copy of the *Big Issue*, the magazine sold by homeless people, and read a full-page feature about one of their senior managers, who was leaving the *Big Issue* to go and work with the Prison Reform Trust. I wrote to her, and found that they were embarking on a campaign to prevent homelessness on release. I was asked to write a scoping study for the campaign, and thus began six years of work for them in various prisons.

Waiting

We will often find that we have to wait for clarity. We are an impatient species, and the Spirit's time is often not our own. In this kind of process, waiting is difficult but seems inevitable, and the waiting needs to be done in an open kind of way, allowing possibilities to enter. We alone cannot make things happen; and old habits based on believing that we can only lead to frustration. Mike said that he has to wait, sometimes months, for confirmation that what he's thinking of is the right thing to do.

This is particularly evident when we find ourselves in a time of transition. Judy Clinton has written of this state,

If we act too quickly out of our fear of being in "don't know" we only superimpose on our lives that which we have already known. If we can have the courage to stay in the not knowing state a new reality will come up out of the circumstances within which we find ourselves.

We have to wait for the moment of possibility, remain committed to action while not being attached to outcomes, recognising when we don't know what is going to happen, when we can't know what the outcome might be. It might be quite different from our imaginings. It might be better. It might be well beyond anything that we might have imagined. We need to begin and trust the process. Open ourselves to unexpected encounters. Allow ourselves to be surprised.

Thy will be done

In our imperfect human state we have to learn to live with unanswered questions.

Obedience to that process means trust, is the very meaning of "faith", the surrender of ambition, plans, decisions made by the ego and the urge to control. This may feel to some like a curbing of freedom, but by freeing ourselves from slavery to our impulses we are gaining a far greater freedom. We need to admit how little we know of the larger scheme of things, to be content in our not knowing, go forward in faith. "Thy will be done" is for me the only prayer of any worth. It will "be done" whether we pray for it or not, but our prayer aligns us with that purpose, marks our acceptance. Obedience to that will, however we discern it, is life's major task, allowing God to work in us. Despite my initial resistance to the word, "obedience" now is for me a fundamental, perhaps the central, part of the sacramental life. With the world inside as our guide, we have moments of choice: to betray our true self or to say "yes".

In our action in the world, if we act from that state of ego-free emptiness we will transform the manner of our working. If we work for others, we will know to expect nothing in return.

We do not know what or whom we will meet that might change our lives, our expectations or our plans and how, if we meet them with all our attention and positive intent, our lives can be transformed. We might describe this process as "making our own luck". Or we might consider the process as more significant.

We might find, as Pink Dandelion says, that "the destination is unimportant; the process of being led and following fruitfully is all. God will take us where we need to go – the big picture will emerge in time: a glimpse or reflection of the republic of heaven."

Let us look at some ways of being in the world that express our trust in this process.

Questions

- How do you make decisions?
- How are you obedient?

7

The creative spirit

I believe that creativity is like electricity. We don't understand how it works... we just use it.

Maya Angelou

I have practised walking meditation occasionally for some years, and found it an aid to mindfulness: walking slowly, meditatively, being aware of each part of my foot as it touches the ground. But only when I discovered a version given by Thich Nhat Hanh did the practice expand into meaningfulness. It begins:

Walk without a destination. Wander aimlessly without arriving, being somewhere rather than going somewhere.

Allowing my feet to take me where they will, allowing the body to take over, was a revelation. And so it can be in life. If we allow randomness a place in our lives, experiment with formlessness, have, for instance, a day without a plan, open ourselves to unforeseen possibilities: that is a challenge that can bring unexpected riches. Straying from the known path even when we have no choice – when we have to follow a diversion because the road is blocked – we come across things we have never seen before.

How much more the case if we choose to take a diversion or don't have a route, a plan, in the first place; if we can, even for a little while, detach ourselves from the known. And as much as possible, let go of time constraints. How would it be if we allowed for it to be an open-ended experience, took off our watches, travelled without a map or a plan? If we let go of the need for an end-point, a destination? If we tried to resist the urge to return to home territory, to the comforting confines of the habitual? If we took joy in the process of discovery? Even took pleasure in getting lost – however scary that might be, and whatever that might mean. The eighteenth-century Hassidic Jew, Rabbi Naham de Braslav, suggests it might be an experience to treasure: "If you don't know the way, don't ask someone who knows it – you might never get lost."

Imagine leaving the day open, with nothing in the diary or on the to-do list, allowing things to emerge as they will. Wander outside and see whom you meet, what you find, what you are moved to explore. Such formlessness feels risky: there is a fear that nothing will happen – indeed – or maybe something unexpected will greet our consciousness. Can we cope with the unexpected? Can we make ourselves vulnerable to the unknown? At the very least, a more fallow day will allow creative thoughts to germinate and at some future time to jump into consciousness.

Improvisation

Improvisation in performance is a particular and deliberate way of departing from the known script. The dictionary definition of "something that is created and performed spontaneously or without preparation" is inadequate and only partially accurate. As any exponent of improvisation in music, comedy or theatre will tell you, a great deal of preparation is necessary, "not", says clarinettist and saxophonist John LaPorta, "in order to play like that but to prepare to allow this magical something that will happen". Most improvisation starts from a known base, with known parameters – in jazz a standard melody, in comedy a suggestion thrown out by the audience. As one improv comedy practitioner said: "In my experience it flows easily when there is a hook or a container – like an attitude or a rule that's imposed so that the structure allows freedom."

What happens afterwards is something else. It's like the moment in a glider when the pilot lets go of the tug aircraft, when release is effected, and the glider is on its own, subject to the vagaries of the currents of the air. Experiences have been described:

In comedy:

It was a wonderful feeling – like moving out of the fog into the sunlight (Marquez).

For me, improv, as with all creativity and possibly all of life/Grace, is a matter of getting out of the way (Tanya).

In music:

What it feels like when it's happening is as if you are watching someone else play. Time, rhythm is of the essence of what it is, what goes on in life. Like the ebb and flow of the sea. The seasons, the flux that goes on. To let it happen. You have to let the conscious mind take a holiday. Let the imagination. Trust it. You have to trust it. If there is any fear at all, it will not happen. It will not appear. It's like a flood that comes out, it's like watching this person pop out, this other thing. The hidden self, this entity that you want to come out (LaPorta).

In contact improvisation dance:

It felt truly liberating, spontaneous, in the flow of the moment. A gift of presence. It was an "out of the head" experience, trusting the divine expression flowing through (Karen).

Once the conscious mind interferes, the moment is lost. Practitioners of various kinds of improvisation agreed:

> If there is one thing you get practice doing in improv, it's in turning off your brain's filters. In improv, there are no bad ideas, you don't hesitate on an impulse – you must charge forward with the scene and be fearless about making mistakes (Marquez).

> My mind is a nuisance when doing Impro. It tries to interfere and plan and control and judge. Yes, especially to judge what I'm doing (Marie).

> If I worry where I am, I get lost. Any value judgements come afterwards not while it's happening (LaPorta).

The creative process

It's not just in performance but in the act of creation itself that a form of surrender is required. Skill, yes, technique, hard work, yes, but also allowing the Spirit room to breathe. Art is a process, a spiritual experience. Few creative artists will not have had the experience that John LaPorta describes above – of being painted, written through. A feeling that the work comes from somewhere else. Edgar Degas reported that "only when he no longer knows what he is doing does the painter do good things".

The "not me doing it" experience is common to practices of healing too. Practitioners of Reiki and other healing processes all say that they are simply tapping into a power that is already there. Far from being exhausted by their ministrations, they are refreshed, renewed, by the mutually nourishing experience. And, they say, anyone can do it. We all have the gift of healing, if we open ourselves to the possibility.

Indeed, what we are talking about is very democratic.

Despite protestations – "I'm not creative" – the creative impulse is not restricted to people who are active in the arts. Creativity describes an approach to the whole of life, allowing playfulness and spontaneity to enter our lives; accepting some slack; letting go of the need to control and direct every move. Creativity is living adventurously.

This democratic source of energy is a central concept in the conflict resolution programme, Alternatives to Violence (AVP). If we are open to it and allow it space, "Transforming Power", as the programme calls it, can enter into the dynamics of a conflict to suggest a way forward that has been previously unseen. Not this, not that, but THIS will bring us into harmony; THIS will give us a win-win resolution.

In conflict, in healing, in everyday life, this is a power open to us all.

Beginner's mind

In my own life, this way of being has so far found expression in two ways. The first is in writing fiction. In non-fiction, the basic content and premise are known. The book will change in the writing, to be sure, and there are times when one has the experience of take-off. Grace is at work in any creative act. But a novel may begin from an image, a character, a scene, even a phrase. And then, it seems, anything might happen. I had known in theory that, in the writing, characters may take over the book; I had no idea of the inter-weaving of things felt and observed, the detritus of conscious and unconscious life. I find I cannot make it happen; I have to allow it to unfold.

The second is in becoming a fool (rather than "clown" which is a limited concept and has all sorts of often negative connotations). I have become part of a community of fools. In the words of our teacher, Angela Halvorson Bogo,

The fool archetype takes us deeper into becoming who we are in essence, each moment and beyond social conditioning... Together we cultivate a field of joyful curiosity. In our innocence we make mistakes, trip over our selves and fall into the poetic one being we are.

There is no planning; we are asked to arrive fresh at every moment and respond to whatever happens. The unexpected is a gift to accept and to be acted on with joy. Again we try to work with what in Zen Buddhism is called Beginner's Mind: have no knowledge of anything, to behave as if from another planet, as if just born in that moment. When I tried to describe this way of being to a musical friend, he said, "Ah, improvisation in life."

Questions

- How do you express your creativity?
- What does it feel like?

8

Practice

If you want a life of prayer, the way to get it is by praying... In prayer we discover what we already have. You start where you are and you deepen what you already have. And you realise that you are already there.

Thomas Merton

To reach a condition of unknowing, our only responsibility is to prepare, to be ready and willing to open ourselves to what might come. In our busy, preoccupied lives, there needs to enter a little pause, a breath; there needs to develop a more spacious consciousness, and a willingness to connect with that that is. We need to move beyond the small world of personal preoccupation and feel the wide connection of being part of a larger whole, part of the natural world, feeling the pulse of the life-force and the significance and mystery of the universe, of which we and even our planet are such small parts.

We need to spend time away from our habitual actions and the tyranny of our thinking mind. Distance ourselves from the assault of information coming at us from every side. Spend time in contemplation of beauty – whether man-made as in art, music or poetry – or in the natural world. In the contemplation of a leaf, a tree, the mountains or the sea, we can leave behind our analytical thinking, not wondering about the why or the how of God or creation but in celebration, in awe, in joy at what is. We stop; we are stilled. If a glimpse, an insight, occurs, that's a bonus. We can't make it happen but in that stillness, in that wordless space, there might form a sense of presence. In contemplating its manifestations we may become aware of the immanence of the Spirit.

Silence

Part of that space – between one wave and the next, between the in breath and the out breath – is silence. Not the silence of trying not to speak, not just the absence of external noise, but the absence of inner noise – all the cacophony of thoughts and impressions with which our minds and lives are filled. If we can let it go, let go too of all images, conceptual or visual, let go of language of any kind, if we can clear these, even for an instant, we might come a little closer to the grand silence of the Divine. Our own silence is an aid to inner stillness, an intentional, listening attention, a tuning in, an alignment.

It is not surprising that silence is a key aspect of the mystical traditions of all religions. We cannot express the inexpressible. Only in silence will we be moved to strip ourselves of our material preoccupations and present ourselves in all our true nakedness. Only in silence will we be able to receive the grace of God. Silence is a way towards God. As the title of Pierre Lacout's little book proclaims, "God is Silence".

Meditation

In the West the practice of meditation is usually an active one, often guided or taking the form of focusing on the scriptures, a prayer word, or a particular image. In the East it is either an emptying, a letting go of any discursive idea, or giving one's whole attention to a formless thing, using a *koan* (enigmatic Zen saying) or mantra.

Insight meditation is an all-encompassing practice, a way to healing, purification, detachment and awareness by concentrating on different parts of the body, or pain of the mind or heart. In that stillness, we may be confronted by what the Buddhists call "the three poisons": craving, hatred and ignorance, which sum up aspects of our negative thinking, and need to be understood and assimilated. Practice is built up over a long period; steadfastness and concentration are the keynotes. What is required is a willingness to let go of everything and go to the centre of our being.

Vipassana meditation is an intensive and repetitive practice of developing mindfulness. The form it took in the Thai meditation monastery that I visited was individual repetitive and timed meditation, walking or sitting slowly and mindfully, stopping to acknowledge any distraction such as an awareness of the senses or a movement of thought, by naming it: "hunger, hunger, hunger" or "sleepy, sleepy, sleepy" until it has passed. No guilt is attached, no sense of "failure", merely an acknowledgement and a new beginning. Ten minutes' walking; ten minutes' sitting, then starting all over again.

Whatever the practice, embarking on the practice of meditation is the ultimate in active unknowing. As we let go of the consciousness of feelings – both emotional and of bodily sensation – and of thoughts, still clinging to the edges of the known and familiar, and allow ourselves to enter into the spacious realm of the unknown: that setting of intention is active unknowing. Robertson quotes Jiddu Krishnamurti who, after many decades of meditation practice, wrote: "A meditative mind is silent. It is not the silence which thought can conceive of; it is not the silence of a still evening; it is the silence when thought – with all its images, its words and perceptions – has entirely ceased."

Prayer

A lot of people have a problem with prayer, even monks whose lives are devoted to prayer, but still talk of going through the motions, and the difficulties of keeping mind and voice in harmony. St Paul expressed the fact that we do not know how to pray. We may not know what, if anything, we are praying to. If we don't know, what is the point of prayer?

What is prayer?

For those who do not have a tradition of liturgy or ritual, and for whom prayer is usually mental, wordless, and often personal, it is hard to define (and to do?). If we accept our lack of knowing, then our whole view of prayer takes on a different meaning. A traditional view of prayer is to ask something of God. In petitionary or supplicatory prayer we pray *for* things, for ourselves or for others. We pray that our wishes be fulfilled. But how do we know what to wish for? We pray that something may happen (or not happen); there is an expectation of an outcome. But what is the right outcome? Who are we to think that we know it? Hard as it may be, our current suffering may be just what is needed for spiritual growth. Prayer of this kind is still making assumptions about our own knowledge; we are still trying to be in control.

Intention

If we let go of that wish to control, we might realise that the outward cause is not changed by prayer. The idea of "praying for" someone or something, when we might consider that all is known to God in any case, seems unhelpful. We do not pray to affect God but that we ourselves might be changed in the process. It is an act of sharing with God, not an attempt to prompt God into action. It is a holding in the Light, both inward and outward. We pray not to God for others but *for* God for them. Prayer is always a commitment. We need to recognise the importance of our involvement, the cost to us. We need to take responsibility for our part in what happens, to allow ourselves to be instruments of God's purpose.

Having left behind the practice of vocal prescribed prayer, for many years I had a problem with the whole idea. It was only when I heard the definition of prayer as "attention" that it began to have meaning for me. As the French mystic, Simone Weil, wrote: "Prayer... is the orientation of all the attention of which the soul is capable towards God." Prayer is an act of faith and will, committing ourselves to the power of focused positive thought or feeling. Prayer is to prepare ourselves, to open ourselves to God's will, and make ourselves channels for God's love, the Spirit. It is a passive state, and many testify to the feeling of not so much praying as being prayed through. Those taking part will be listening not talking, and may feel that they are waiting upon God in prayer. Prayer of this kind is not a formality or an obligation but a place.

Spontaneous

Then there is prayer as a movement of the heart, which may lead to calling out in spontaneous appeal. I sometimes think that that unthinking reaching out is the time when I come closest to God. It's a time when I and my consciousness are out of the way, when I stand naked in my need.

Life as prayer

> *Wherever there is love, there is only prayer. When our heart is in the right place and brimming with love, everything becomes prayer* (Steindl-Rast, 78).

To live our faith is to try to live constantly in the presence of God, to keep that awareness in all that we do, in contemplation of the Presence within and without. A constant receiving and giving. Brother Lawrence, a seventeenth-century French lay brother, wrote a slim little volume of letters and essays called *The Practice of the Presence of God*, describing his life in just such a way: doing everything, every small thing, for the love of God.

A monk told me that "prayer is not so much a matter of words or ideas but rather a deep, inarticulate longing for one in whom one's whole being can rest and be at peace". In the end, it is important to "pray as you can, not as you can't".

Questions

- What is your spiritual practice?
- How does silence affect you?

Reclaiming the dark

All mystery is about the dark. All darkness is about mystery.
Matthew Fox

Darkness gets a bad press. It is light that is used to describe experiences of inspiration and transformation; dark by extension is the opposite of that. A friend described the prevalent attitude as "cosmic racism"!

The word does of course have negative connotations. The dark can indeed suggest experiences of suffering, death, evil, or our shadow side. We must not underestimate the relentless pain of those who dwell in that state. But for those who emerge from even the darkest of those times, an experience can be transformative. Suffering, however unable or unwilling we are to see it at the time, can lead to an opening up. It is commonplace for people to find greater understanding, to be able to access a different dimension, through being cracked open by trauma. (In Leonard Cohen's words, "There is a crack in everything; that's how the light gets in.") The access of faith at such times is not a search for comfort, but a result of the newly created space that enables it to enter.

We all have periods of dryness. In times of darkness and apparent lack of progress, the internal work continues. The dark is a place of growth. We can sometimes look back on periods of seeming sterility to find that that fallow time was necessary for later development. In the darkness of the earth plants germinate, seeds develop, fallow ground is renewed. We ourselves began in darkness. For nine months we lay in the womb, and developed all the extraordinary complexities of our human being.

The American priest and former Dominican, Matthew Fox, has spoken of the necessity of reclaiming the dark. During our lives, periods of emptiness, dryness, passivity, can provide a springboard for inspiration and decisive energy. Solutions to problems can sometimes appear without effort after a good night's sleep. In creative activities, it is often the pondering time that is most fruitful; in my own writing, I know that a blank day when nothing seems to work can be followed by the emergence of creative energy.

You could say that darkness is the visual equivalent of silence: a condition that creates the possibility of space and openness, and an opportunity for listening. During a recent stay in a hotel my bedroom was, I found, a place that afforded complete darkness. When I switched off the light I could see nothing. Even when my eyes had adjusted to the dark, it was possible to lie on my back with eyes open and see nothing. At such times, like the vast featureless spaces of the desert, that "nothing" seems full: of infinite potential, infinite space. The darkness does not close in, rather the spirit expands towards infinity. Shutting our eyes, as many do during worship, will remove visual distraction and aid the journey within, but sitting in the dark with eyes open can extend that realm beyond the boundaries of self.

Not knowing

Above all, the dark is a metaphor for our not knowing. The dark has become a metaphor of ignorance not only in ordinary life – "I'm in the dark" – but in the spiritual dimension.

By "darkness" I mean "a lack of knowing" – just as anything that you do not know or may have forgotten may be said to be "dark" to you, for you cannot see it with your inner eye. For this reason it is called "a cloud", not of the sky, of course, but "of unknowing", a cloud of unknowing between you and your God (*Cloud*, 58).

The metaphor is also in common use in the world of science. As Oliver Robinson says in his work in progress, *Paths between head and heart: How science and spirituality relate*,

> Recently scientists have found that much of the universe, maybe the majority, is composed of dark matter and dark energy, both of which are currently invisible to all scientific instruments. Dark matter is everywhere but passes through normal matter without interacting with it. We currently have no idea what the world of dark matter is like and what goes on within it... Science is now being forced to accept that great swathes of reality are beyond its reach, at least for now. It has bumped into the transcendent, and called anything to do with it "dark".

Proceeding in that darkness is an expression of trust, of faith. It is not surprising that "trust" games usually entail shutting our eyes and relying on others to lead us, or catch us as we fall. Walking in complete darkness can be frightening. As with faltering steps we make our way, it is hard not to be debilitated by fear, ostensibly of bumping into something, tripping over a hole or a root, but perhaps more profoundly by our fear of the unknown.

> Art thou in the Darkness? Mind it not, for if thou dost it will fill thee more, but stand still and act not, and wait in patience till Light arises out of Darkness to lead thee (James Nayler, ?1617-1660).

"The dark night of the soul" is a phrase that has come to be used in a general way to describe a spiritual crisis, but has its more precise origins in a poem by Saint John of the Cross. We will look more closely at what it means in the final chapters of this book.

Questions

- How does darkness affect you?
- Is trust a problem?

10

Acceptance

But there is a deeper, an internal simplification of the whole of one's personality, stilled, tranquil, in childlike trust listening ever to Eternity's whisper, walking with a smile into the dark.

Thomas Kelly

At the heart of resistance to not knowing is fear and a sense of insecurity. It's hard to move away from the known, the familiar, in any sphere of our lives. In our worship it is hard to free ourselves, perhaps, from dogma and familiar structures, and allow for the unpredictability of a dynamic Spirit. Allow for the possibility of change. In our working lives it's hard to face financial insecurity to pursue what we know to be our mission. There are few who can follow Jesus' teaching that like the lilies of the field we consider not the morrow, but trust that all will be given. I know one or two who can and do, but they are rare souls. In any circumstance, it's frightening to realise that we are not in control.

Anxiety propels us into an imagined future that will probably never exist. We worry about what might happen; anxiety about possible failures or mishaps fill our waking and sometimes our dreaming lives. But anxiety or worry about outcomes is not only pointless, it is a symptom of a lack of trust. Brother Lawrence didn't even prepare for tasks, just entrusted them to God, and he knew that all would be well. The mediaeval anchoress, Julian of Norwich, also knew in the core of her being that "all shall be well. All manner of things shall be well." But belief of this kind is not some starry-eyed Pollyanna-ish naiveté but in both these people was grounded in an inner peace developed over years of experience, struggle and suffering.

It's only when our discomfort with the status quo and our need for freedom are greater than our fear that we might be prepared to open ourselves to an unknown outcome. At the heart of faith is "a personal commitment to go further, perseverance in relationship with what is not yet fully known to us but which we gradually realise is the source of all knowledge" (Laurence Freeman). We need to trust. We need to pay attention and be open to promptings from a power just waiting for our response. We need to be open to the advent of grace – one of the most beautiful words in the language. As Fr Freeman has said, grace is "a force from beyond the horizon of our own will". A gift, freely given, and not according to our deserts.

Not knowing is at the centre of spiritual life. It is only by creating a space in which anything can happen that we allow God to speak; only by stepping back that we allow space for that unpredictable Spirit that brings us gifts beyond any of our imaginings. Without that space, we are wedded to our habitual expectations and busyness, our ego-enhancing preoccupations. We can't hear; we can't listen. "God", says the Benedictine Abhishiktananda, "dwells only where man steps back to give him room."

Accepting not knowing as a way is not about fatalism, or living in some passive state. We need to be passive to God in our listening, but this is in order to receive guidance about how to be active to the world. Acceptance is not giving into helplessness, or any notion that we can't make a difference. It is about following our passion, our sense of what is right, discerning how we are meant to be, what we are meant to be doing, while listening to the small voice within and being open to what might actually happen.

Opening ourselves to risk and unpredictability in this way takes us to a place of vulnerability – but also to what John

O'Donohue calls "a continuous undertow of possibility". It opens us to a fuller experience of all that life brings us, and a closer relationship with the created world. When we accept that the nature of God can't be discovered through cognitive knowing, it frees us to seek without a goal. When we accept that we can't know what will happen, it enables us to go forward in trust, and in faith that the right course of action will be shown.

It is in the walking that our path is revealed.

There is no secret to success. Simply go forward with awareness. Your path is unknown and unseen, until you walk it. Only your steps forward reveal it.

Ellen Grace O'Brian

Thy word is a lamp unto my feet
And a light unto my path

Psalm 119:105

Many of us may have had experiences of letting go, of allowing ourselves to be guided, and know the freedom and clarity that that gives us. But staying in that place of ego-free trust is another matter. Gordon Matthews has commented on the quote from Thomas Kelly that opens this chapter:

How can we walk with a smile into the dark? We must learn to put our trust in God and the leadings of the Spirit. How many of us are truly led by the Spirit throughout our daily lives? I have turned to God when I have had a difficult decision to make or when I have sought strength to endure the pain in dark times. But I am only slowly learning to dwell in the place where leadings come from. That is a place of love and joy and peace, even in the midst of pain. The more I dwell in that place, the easier it is to smile, because I am no longer afraid.

If we dwell in the presence of God, we shall be led by the spirit. We do well to remember that being led by the spirit depends not so much upon God, who is always there to lead us, as upon our willingness to be led. We need to be willing to be led into the dark as well as through green pastures and by still waters. We do not need to be afraid of the dark, because God is there. The future of this earth need not be in the hands of the world's "leaders". The world is in God's hands if we are led by God. Let us be led by the Spirit. Let us walk with a smile into the dark.

Questions

- What are you afraid of?
- What is your experience of being guided?

The Cloud of Unknowing

My head is bursting
with the joy of the unknown.
My heart is expanding a thousand fold.
Every cell,
taking wings,
flies about the world.
All seek separately
the many faces of my Beloved.

Hush Don't Say Anything to God: Passionate Poems of Rumi
(1999), translated by Shahram Shiva

What we have considered so far is only the beginning. Now we enter the heart of the matter. It is in our approach to the Divine that the whole state and practice of unknowing are fulfilled.

Most of us live an active life largely unconscious of the transcendental dimension. In general our attention is focused on the preoccupations of daily life, our consciousness punctuated only occasionally by withdrawal, a retreat, or a moment of self-remembrance. For some the yearning for presence will lead to a more rigorous prayer life, a willingness to strip away the trappings of ordinary life to enter more often into silent communion with the unknowable. Withdrawal becomes a habit; solitude a necessity, the universe of silent listening an extension of ourselves.

In such periods of spiritual practice we may catch the occasional glimpse of something beyond, may even have what is referred to as a "peak experience", an enhanced perception of reality, when the boundaries between ourselves and the outside world are blurred, merged, when time vanishes and we feel the presence of the eternal in that moment, the infinite in that place. As the *Cloud* author says, these moments are brief and unexpected: "It is always a sudden impulse and comes without warning, springing up to God like some spark from the fire" (57). But for most of us those moments will not be the mainstay of the spiritual life. Indeed, a Vipassana teacher warned me against the dangers of attachment to such experiences. "After the ecstasy comes the laundry".

But in some cases such an event is life-changing. Once we experience such a suspension of "normal" life, once we know that that can happen, it is inevitable that we will look for a recurrence, and that we will consciously or unconsciously create an environment in which it is more likely to happen. Undergoing the experience will in itself alter our perceptions of the world, what we expect from it, and how we approach it.

What is difficult is to carry the understanding and experience from these glimpses into the rest of life, to hold in balance such disparate ways of being. Thomas Kelly writes well of attempting to live an integrated life.

"There is", he says:

...a way of ordering our mental life on more than one level at once. On one level, we may be thinking, discussing, seeing, calculating, meeting all the demands of external affairs. But deep within, behind the scenes, at a profounder level, we may also be in prayer and adoration, song and worship and a gentle receptiveness to divine breathings (35).

This is as far as most of us will go. But, according to Evelyn Underhill, "This acknowledgement of our intellectual ignorance, this humble surrender, is the entrance into the

'Cloud of Unknowing', *the first step* towards mystical knowledge of the Absolute" (348, my italics). It is not enough to acknowledge how little we know and let go of the need to know; it is not enough even to let go of being ruled by cognitive reasoning. What the *Cloud* author asks us to do is not just about not knowing and acknowledging our ignorance, but actively "un-knowing": stripping ourselves of what we do know, leaving behind all our sensory experience, even any previous experience or concept of God, even the awareness of our own existence, under what he calls "a Cloud of Forgetting". Only when the heart and the will are focused entirely on a desire for God will transformation be possible.

Underhill divides the process of spiritual development into five stages: awakening, purgation (including waiting in grounded stillness, simplicity and silence) and illumination. Then comes what St John of the Cross described as "the dark night of the soul" – a purging of all that gets in the way of the complete surrender to God that comes in the fifth stage: the stage of unselfing.

Can we attain this state in this life? Won't our bodily self simply fall away? The *Cloud* author sees life as having four levels: two active and two contemplative levels with the higher active level overlapping the lower contemplative. The higher contemplative level is, he says, not accessible in our lifetime – he feels it is not possible to stay under the Cloud of Forgetting all the time. Suppressing our knowledge of everything may be possible for split seconds, or short periods in meditation. It is not possible, he says, to be fully contemplative on earth without being active.

Nonetheless, the accounts of such mystics as St John of the Cross and Julian of Norwich reveal a life very close to this unitive higher level. Happold distinguishes a rare breed of human who have both the spiritual gifts and the complete commitment, who are not content with practising contemplation, but entering into a *state* of contemplation. Such a state of consciousness is, as Happold says, rare: it is outside the realm of normal experience. Happold describes their experience as "a movement of consciousness towards a higher level, as the result of the emergence and cultivation of powers which in most men and women remain latent".

A state of contemplation, he says, is a more "developed form of that inward turning towards the deep centre of the soul". In that state is found "a self-forgetting attention, a humble receptiveness, a still and steady gazing, an intense concentration, so that emotion, will, and thought are all fused and then lost in something that is none of them, but which embraces them all" (69-70). It is in this state of contemplation that the ultimate kind of knowing is to be found, a knowing in which there is no division between the knower and the known, into which the multiplicities of the human being are merged into the oneness of the Divine. All is one.

Despite the difficulty of describing any such experience, some of those who have been prepared to give up all in a total commitment to a pursuit of union with God have left us accounts of extraordinary vividness. On this earth they remained, but in general they renounced the world and lived apart. There are exceptions: in the Sufi tradition the aspirant "is bidden to plunge into the world, to merge himself in it, so that he may be able to understand what it truly is" (Happold, 249).

Love

By love he can be caught and held, but by thinking never.
                                        The Cloud of Unknowing

We have considered the various ways in which we cannot know; we have looked at a different kind of knowing; but when we approach the question of how we can "know" God, the only answer seems to be by love.

In a discussion of God, the word "love" is never far away. I used to have a real problem with the idea that God loved me. I felt a lot of things about and from God, but I did not feel loved. It was only when I realised that I was nurtured, not with the cuddly limited love of my imaginings but in a quite different way, that I came to experience its truth. I realised that love – like God, so far beyond my own understanding – embraces me as a unique part of the interconnected universe, loves me with a mature and all-encompassing acceptance of my real self. Grace is the expression of that love: only because God loved us first are we able to access faith and to understand what loving God and loving others might mean.

As the poems of Rumi and the Song of Solomon bear witness, human love is an ancient metaphor for the relationship with the Divine, a way of channelling our fumbling efforts to express the inexpressible. In a moving and thought-provoking discussion at the Royal Society of Arts on the subject of "What is the love that I need?", the contributions from the two speakers covered many aspects of love, but in talking of one kind of love, the others were never absent. In answer to the question "Does love come out of the relationship itself, or from something that is already there?" Devorah Baum said: "While I'm yearning, transcendence is always on the menu". She talked of how love "hurtles us towards the other, the stranger, the unknown," in whom we would lose or find ourselves. "Love", she said, "shares with faith a relationship with the unknown." Shares too that experience of falling, of an action beyond our control.

The thirteenth-century mystic, Mechtild of Magdeburg, laid great emphasis on the primacy of love, considering it to be the last lesson that she learnt in the wilderness. She felt that there was "a vital link between love and knowledge" (Anderson, 131).

Someone once asked, "What is love?"

"Be lost in me," I said. "You'll know love when that happens."

Love has no calculating in it. That's why it's said to be a quality of God and not of human beings. "God loves you" is the only possible sentence. The subject becomes the object so totally that it can't be turned around. Who will the "you" pronoun stand for, if you say, "You love God"?

Rumi (274)

This is Love: to fly heavenward,
To rend, every instant, a hundred veils,
The first moment, to renounce life;
The last step, to fare without feet.
To regard this world as invisible,
Not to see what appears to oneself.

Jalalu 'd Din, in Underhill (348)

Or as Julian of Norwich has it:

What, do you want to know your lord's meaning in this thing? Know it well, love was his meaning. Who reveals it to you? Love. What did he reveal to you? Love. Why does he reveal it to you? For love.

in Mitchell, 128-29

Love is both a noun and a verb; both the feeling and the act. As Baum says, "We *are* that yearning for the other." And if God is love? Being, doing, noun, verb, God and love are the ground of our being, there on the path of unknowing for us to find, both the destination and the way.

Questions

- Have you experienced a sense of presence?
- How do you experience love?

Further Reading and Resources

Anderson, Elizabeth, "'With the eyes of my soul': Mechtild of Magdeburg's experiences" in *Friends Quarterly*, July 2006

Anonymous, translated into modern English by Clifton Wolters, *The Cloud of Unknowing*. Harmondsworth: Penguin, 1961

Fox, Matthew, *Original Blessing*. Santa Fe: Bear & Co, 1983

Happold, F.C., *Mysticism*. Harmondsworth: Penguin, 1970

Huxley, Aldous, *The Perennial Philosophy*. London: Chatto & Windus, 1946

James, William, *The Varieties of Religious Experience: A Study in Human Nature*. Harmondsworth: Penguin, 1985

Jarman, Roswitha, *Breakthrough to Unity*. London: The Kindlers, 2010

Kelly, Thomas, *A Testament of Devotion*. NY: HarperCollins, 1992

Lacout, Pierre, *God is Silence*. London: Quaker Books, 2005

Lane, Beldon C. *The Solace of Fierce Landscapes*. Oxford: Oxford University Press, 1998

Laporta, John, https://www.youtube.com/watch?v=AUizgbioHOU

Marquez, Amy, http://boxesandarrows.com/the-creative-impact-of-improvization/

Merton, Thomas, *The Intimate Merton*. Oxford: Lion publishing, 2000

Mitchell, Stephen (ed.), *The Enlightened Mind*. New York: HarperCollins, 1993

Robinson, Oliver, *Paths between head and heart: how science and spirituality relate*. Work in progress

Rowson, Jonathan and McGilchrist, Iain, *Divided Brain, Divided World*. London: RSA, 2013

Rumi. *The Essential Rumi*, trans. Coleman Barks. London: Penguin, 1995

Steindl-Rast, David, *The Music of Silence*. Berkeley Ca: Seastone, 1998

Tolle, Eckhart, *Stillness Speaks*. London: Hodder and Stoughton, 2003

Underhill, Evelyn, *Mysticism*. Oxford: Oneworld Publications, 1994

Wolff, Milo, in http://www.quantummatter.com/

The World is our Cloister

The dedicated religious life of monks and nuns has a fascination for many of us – at a distance. We live in the world we have, and it's hard to figure out how to do it in a God-filled way. *The World is our Cloister* is about the new religious life: a life to which a Protestant, Catholic, Hindu or those with no label can relate. It is a guide to living the devotional life, not behind the walls of a monastery, but in the world. It's about engagement in the world as well as withdrawal, the balance between a life of action and one of contemplation. It is also a guide to the mystical experience at the heart of all religion. Beyond the barriers of belief and practice lies the stark and simple reality of relating to God: the practice of the presence of God.

"A beautiful book. One would have to be spiritually dead not to find a very great deal here which is worth reading - and putting into practice." *Faith and Freedom*; "A very good and thought-provoking book." Susan Hill: "Jennifer writes poetically and with great wisdom… a book which is a balm for the soul – a grace-filled book." Lucinda Vardey, author of *God in All Worlds*, etc.

Jennifer is a former literary agent, now a community worker, a writer, and an active, as well as contemplative, Quaker.

978-1-84694-049-1 (Paperback) £11.99 $24.95

Simplicity Made Easy

In folk history and religion, from the Shakers to Zen, we see the importance of simplicity. The appeal of living more simply may be to leave a smaller carbon footprint, to express a compassionate solidarity with those who have least, or simply to downsize. Whatever our own motivation, it is likely to spring from within.

At heart, simplicity is a focus on what matters. Reducing the clutter in our lives, whether in material objects or in use of time or money, leads to an increased clarity of vision. Step by step, we can move towards a state in which our attitudes and life are made one. Simplicity is the outward and visible sign of an inward and spiritual grace.

Simplicity is more than a lifestyle option: it is a way of life.

Jennifer Kavanagh gave up her career as a literary agent to work in the community. In 2003 she gave up most of her possessions. Jennifer is a Quaker and this is her fourth book.

978-1-84694-543-4 (Paperback) £4.99 $9.95

CHRISTIAN
ALTERNATIVE

Throughout the two thousand years of Christian tradition there
have been, and still are, groups and individuals that exist in the
margins and upon the edge of faith. But in Christianity's
contrapuntal history it has often been these outcasts and
pioneers that have forged contemporary orthodoxy out of
former radicalism as belief evolves to engage with and
encompass the ever-changing social and scientific realities. Real
faith lies not in the comfortable certainties of the Orthodox, but
somewhere in a half-glimpsed hinterland on the dirt track to
Emmaus, where the Death of God meets the Resurrection, where
the supernatural Christ meets the historical Jesus, and where the
revolution liberates both the oppressed and the oppressors.

Welcome to Christian Alternative... a space at the edge where
the light shines through.